Readers' Comments

"Humorous, soulful, and thoroughly accessible, this book invites the reader to... see life from an extraordinary perspective." - Julie Maechler, Professor of English Literature, Ventura, CA.

"Those who have experienced emotional growth through pain in their lives will find meaning here... a touch of humor along with the metaphor makes it delightful..." - Connie Haessler, adoption counselor, Pittsburgh, PA.

"Jackie Bach's poems are witty and wry, funny and sad, and the line drawings complement them perfectly. You will find something special for you in them, and something that gives you a totally new insight." - Emmon W. Bach, Professor Emeritus of Linguistics, University of Massachusetts.

Brain Storms

by

Jackie Bach

with illustrations
by the author

Printed by Kimberly Press, Inc. 1998

ACKNOWLEDGMENTS

I wish to give David Bach my heartfelt thanks for his great belief in my work and for his unflagging support in so many ways. And a special thank you goes to Julie Maechler, my greatest critic and sounding board, for her diligent help in keeping this book in focus. Also, I would like to thank the many readers of my first book, <u>Through The Bach Door</u>, who encouraged me to write a second book.

*To my family
with love
and thanks.*

New Beginnings

Beginning
a new chapter
blank page
writer's block
head against a rock.
Fingers drum upon the desk
a certain fear creeps in:
will I write today? tomorrow?
ever again?
Ideas in molasses
try to lift their sticky feet.
I wad some paper
make some coffee
(which I never drink)
and watch a spider on the wall
fill its blank page surely,
with precision.
No hesitation there,
for its decision has been made.
But, as lovely
as its shimmering webs may be,
they stay the same
time after time
while mine . . .
. . . I pick up my pen and write.

First Born

With freckles and specs
and thick curly hair
hanging over,
the "little professor"
lived with us.
He penned his stories
and clever cartoons
from deep within
a funny bone
that reached across his pain,
that reached across our hearts.
And
all too soon he grew up,
and from within a messy room,
(which I now miss),
he walked out into the world,
walked out into his future.
But
in a way, he never left,
for the stories and the memories
still remain, gentle smiles
that live within.

Omelets

Mothers and daughters
are a scramble,
a sticky tangle of emotions.
And I swear
that being both
hasn't helped me figure out
one bit
how to tread upon these fragile
paths of eggshells
without cracking up.
It's just a good thing
I like omelets!

Broken Thoughts

Thoughts of her have shattered
like fine crystal
dropped upon a marble floor.
Those splintered pieces,
silent broken cameos,
gaze blankly up at me:
dead eyes in a pale relief
and sullen lips in half-smile frozen,
till I sweep them from my floor.
I cup them in my bleeding hand,
much too precious to throw out
and too painful to ignore.

Father Was a Baker

Father, dear,
you kneaded me
with worn hands
heavy with fatigue
and
placed me in a bowl
to rise to your occasion.
You shaped me day by day
to follow
in your floured footsteps.
But, just before
you popped me in the oven
to get me hard-crusted
(just like you)
I rolled away and
hopped into an oven
of my own choosing.
Same result?
I wonder. . . .

Not Belonging

Not belonging
sometimes feels
so heavy on the chest,
and brings on paranoia
couched in tears.
I thought I had it licked
in all these many years,
and yet behind that grin,
I must admit I still don't
fit that well
in grown-up skin.

Summer Solstice
(6/21/97)

Summer,
officially crowned today,
majestically twirls
in radiant robes,
enchanting us
with
her grace
and strength,
her beauty
and bright laughter.
But, secretly
she's clutching her days
like an old
tightfisted moneylender.
Regardless,
they will slowly shrink
before her eyes,
and one by one
slip out between her fingers
as she journeys powerless
toward the winter.

The Musicians

The musicians
hold their instruments aloft,
drawing forth the notes
so softly
that they gently flow
upon the air.
Then slowly,
rich crescendos swell and
tumble out
   upon us
      like cascading waterfalls
quenching thirst below,
reviving those who listen
with parched souls.

The Old Baldwin

The old Baldwin
sits silent and unused
in the lady's parlor
as the ghosts of students past
and the mistress
and the music that they made
yet mingle
in the still and dusty air.

Sea of Faces

Undulating sea of faces
every shape and color floating
caught unguarded
in this freeze frame of our history -
weary faces of the world
unfolding and uniting,
drawn into one countenance
of grief, with teardrops falling
in that stream of our mortality,
that river which will sweep
us all away from earthly ties
one day - we who yet remain and
walk upon its cloudy banks.
And so,
we grieve not just for her,
dear "Queen of Hearts",
but for ourselves as well.

The Healing Power of Poetry

Often it feels like
I'm grabbed by the hair
dragged to my room
and plunked in my chair
where I sit for hours in another world
honing words and thoughts
that funnel through raw feelings.
And by this method
(blood-letting in the mind)
I sometimes find a truth about myself
I didn't know before or couldn't face.
I hold it underneath the glass
and strip it bare -
still afraid to scrutinize,
but learning slowly
how to separate the truth from lies.

Searching

Searching
through the hills and valleys
of your face,
that wondrous place
where you reside,
I recognized a landscape
not unlike my own.
And moving closer
to the onyx pools,
what did I find?
That the pain I saw
reflected there was mine.

Pieces of Myself

Pieces of myself
hang like tatters
from a rag doll
lifeless
in the closet
waiting
for some miracle
of reassembly.
Do you see this scattered me -
ears on a hanger
lips on the shelf, and
elbows draped over
the hatrack?
My desires hang with the belts,
and contemplations
fold themselves
in with the sweaters.
Dark fears hide in pockets,
and my silly old heart
is on my sleeve
where it's always been -
tacked on with ragged stitches.

At Stearn's Wharf

As the sun slips down
dragging the day along with it,
the clouds begin to blush
mirrored in a fountain flowing,
color spreading over edges
slowly,
silently in strips.
A graceful porpoise arcs above,
frozen mid-dive,
with his bright metallic eyes
wide open,
as if caught there by surprise.

The Tattoos
(Etchings From the Soul)

The tattoo
on her shoulder's like
a magic marker butterfly
except the ink won't wash away.
But, it's not the bolder of the two,
for that flaming heart upon her rear's
more shocking
(and it's also prob'ly more sincere),
although that skin is hidden
from most probing eyes
my dear.

Ideas Drip

Ideas drip
off the slip of a tongue
rolling sticky
stubborn
out of mullioned windows
in a mind that
snap-crackle-pops
nonstop
as chemicals collide and
intertwine
giving us sometimes
a few distilled, pure drops
but more often
thick and dirty
dredged-up-from-the-
basement thoughts.

Where Day Is Night

In a land
where day is night
where the earth and sky unite
into a thin, white line,
all who try to live there
are entombed
within themselves,
within this hostile land.

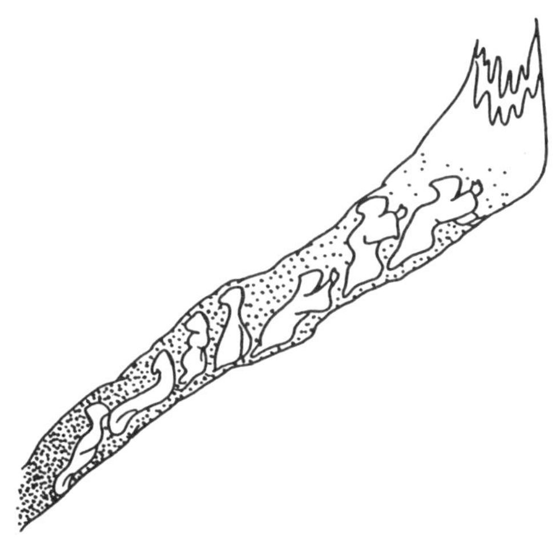

In the Valley of the Dolls

In the valley of the dolls
where heads roll limply
on pale shoulders,
and where glassy eyes
stare deeply
into fractured worlds,
thoughts curl inward
searching for an answer,
or at least
a moment's peace.
But even though
the lids may close
in this pharmaceutical
promised land,
there is no rest;
there is no dreamless sleep.

The Physicists
(Safety in Numbers?)

They hide behind
their glasses
and their strings
of calculations,
their world defined
in particles and numbers -
a world to which
the rest of us are blind.

Tankers

Tankers
squat and square
slumber in the harbor fog,
their dented hulls
at rest.
Snug and safe,
they're unaware
of storms now howling
in the channel,
and do not care
one toot
about their rusty bottoms.

The Fishermen

The fishermen
unload
their rusty boat,
not a thing of beauty,
(never was),
and the belly yields
its dead,
amid thick smells
of rotting sea
and diesel smoke,
amid the cries of gulls
and men.

He Is Gone

He is gone.
I think we won't
be friends again.
But even so, he lingers,
churning in my mind
along with all those
unkind words he shot
into my heart,
jagged arrows dipped
in hatred.
That he doesn't love me
anymore,
oh, I realize it now,
deep inside old bones
grown cold.
He is gone.

Tongues

Tongues
pinkly lick
and taste,
talk of love
or lash out hate.
They spit out words
in hot debate,
forming
sticky
fricatives:

Mirrors Are Unfriendly

Mirrors are unfriendly.
They hit you
right between the eyes
with lies:
spots and bags and wrinkles.
I'm aghast at what I see -
an older woman's looking
back at me, some other.
I can't believe it's me,
because she looks just like
my mother!

This Birthday

This birthday
lies in wait -
there is no escape.
Believe me,
I don't want it,
but I can't hide from it
can't run from it
can't stuff it
or snuff it,
so I'm stuck with it.
(Please bring cake!)

The Night Was Coming On

The night was coming on
inside and out
and I drifted in a blood-red fog.
But I do remember begging her
to drive me to that place of safety,
silent but for keys
that twisted in their locks,
silent but for screams
that cut the night air like a knife,
slicing toward the dawn's red light
and dull pale winter days
behind closed doors.
And I stood frozen there in fear
without a pen, a plan or a shoelace.
Yes, the night was coming on
inside and out, and
I still remember.

No One Listens

At a party
people talk
till throats grow raw
and eyes glaze over,
but no one really listens.
I think I'll give up parties,
stay at home
and talk to my cats.
They listen.

Beads of Piety

Beads of piety
glistened on her brow,
partly hidden underneath
the netting of her pillbox hat,
the old one that she wore
on Sundays (and at funerals).
But, by early Monday
those same beads had dried
and blown away,
taking all her piety with them.
She began her workweek
crabby and perturbed,
forgetting once again
the "good news"
that she heard the day before.
But,
Sunday soon will come again,
and she will be there
with her beads.
Amen.

We Have Grown Afraid

We have grown afraid to touch
each other
except through rubber-gloved
appendages.
But, even though we're quite protected
all around the edges,
we can still be
deeply touched inside sometimes,
behind our walls of fear and prejudice.

In Group

I watch them with a jaundiced eye,
all broken people like myself
patients not so patient anymore
yet waiting in a quiet circle,
hoping still for miracles,
their downcast eyes now lifting
nervously,
ears attuned to crisp steps
halting at the open doorway:
the doctor (god) is in!
I look around and wonder
if they're thinking
what I'm thinking:
Is it possible that this young and
clean-scrubbed
bright-eyed "doctor-child"
could ever understand - let alone
begin to heal - the pain?

Brain Cells

They're called brain "cells"
because the memories
    locked within are "lifers" -
(unless something goes
    amiss),
        for no minimum
        security
        prison,
        this.

Roller Coaster

This roller coaster sometimes
sucks the life out
scares the pie out
jerks me up-down bumpy tracks
leaves me flushed and breathless
screams a-tumbling
lost within the wind.
Fingers reach out frantically
to rake the emptiness in passing -
nothing there to hold me steady
on this one-way trip.
I sometimes think
the ride is going to come full circle,
stop
or at least slow down, but
around some hidden bend
it all begins again,
and I can't get off!

The Verdict

The doctors gave him little hope.
With helpless hands that scratched
their furrowed brows,
they didn't know quite how
to tell him he was dying.
(Don't they practice this in school?)
Instead, they hemmed and hawed
and shifted weight like nervous
adolescent school boys,
even though
they must've handed down this
verdict countless times before.
With vacant eyes
that wouldn't look at his
but focused on the door,
(like deer eyes caught
within a headlight beam),
I wondered if they heard
the screaming locked beneath
his silent skin. I know I did.

The Silence of Goodbye

I knew before
the doctors came
and made it all official
in their starched white coats,
and paper signed
with cause of death
and time.
(And who, I wonder, really
cares about all that?).
Before the dawn,
in that timeless
and fluorescent place,
he and I both knew
we had to face the silence
of goodbye.
He finally did escape
those pale green walls,
slipping through them
and my fingers,
casting off his earthly crown,
casting off for parts unknown.

Mind Bounce

My mind
bounces
like a rubber ball
on concrete.
And it doesn't care at all
upon which street it
bounces.

The Opportunity

The opportunity
came knocking
at my door,
sat shiny and neglected
on the floor until
it rolled behind a chair.
I left it there.
And being young
and foolish then,
I quite forgot about it.
Well, I needed it
the other day,
and searched the room
where it had lain
forgotten many years.
A dusty object
caught my eyes
and only then I realized
exactly what I'd blown:
the opportunity
had turned to stone.

Origins

Can't stop wondering
who I am.
Can't ask the old ones -
they are dead.
Can't separate fact
from fiction anymore.
But
I <u>can</u> check the mirror
and begin to see
the strong survivors
that are me,

staring back

staring back

staring back

staring back

staring back,

Butter

The heavy cream
 which rises to the top
  of my imagination
   often churns itself
    right into butter.

Jello

Jello wiggles like gigolos
 belly-laughing from
  deep within green molds,
   holding on for dear life
    among the nuts
     and cottage cheese.

I Thought If I Could Live

I thought if I could live
inside a cave
that had no mirrors,
no tomorrows,
maybe then I'd find
some peace of mind,
for time would not exist.
The only hint of life would be
the beating of my heart.
I did retreat into a cave of sorts,
one of rock that lay within
and held me up
when I began to fall.
And in my feelings of despair,
the rock
was always there.
But, I found it hard
to hug a rock.

A Matter of Principle

Ensconced in lace
she stumbles and weaves
down the street
in the wee hours,
heels à la "click-clack".
With bottle in hand
she eventually lands
intact upon her doorstep.
And in the morning
ticklish tongues will wag
up and down the street
in the bright glare
of her headache -
her neighbors just as
indiscreet as she,
as they roll this "shameful"
(and delicious) morsel
on their tongues,
this meat that fuels
their idle curiosity,
as they gossip over
morning coffee.

Leaping Decibels

Screaming heads (live and canned),
rap and rock - their music jams.
Jackhammers jump and drill the mind
while sirens wail and traffic whines,
assaulting us in "cacophonic" stereo.
No longer can we sit in peace
and contemplate,
'cause no bucolic state exists,
even in our minds.
For even during quiet moments
on the outside, dear,
we are deafened by the ringing
in our ears!

Coming of Age

We flung ourselves upon the world
like Frisbees:
soaring, flying high
on strong emotional winds,
for we were young then,
and impetuous,
cocky and irreverent.
But when you died
and left us standing there alone,
to sprinkle earth and prayers
upon your grave,
I walked away and
left the passion of my youth,
for it had sealed itself in stone.

Casey Cat

I see her walking by
and call her name.
I think "pad, pad"
for I can't hear
her silent tread.
Her golden moon eyes
gaze at me
reading every nuance
of my mood,
collecting every sign
upon my face
to carefully store behind
her soft approach.
And startled by this
sudden insight of her ways,
I now remember long ago
I lived the same sad way:
with fear behind it all.

Rumblings And Dry Heaves

Sitting in a room too dark and quiet
while an artificial stream
outside his window fails to soothe
my ragged mind with its gurgles,
I try to pull the words out of my mouth
in answer to his probing questions.
Gagging, spitting out
what must be "truth",
throwing up my childhood in small
undigested chunks till nothing's left
but aching emptiness and dry heaves,
I sit exhausted, stuck in that gray area
halfway between "was born and will die"
becoming a cold wind howling
all around his questions,
his Persian carpet, and the impressionistic
paintings on the wall.
He calls it a "watershed" session.
I call it a "breaking-the-head" lesson,
as I mentally leap from the fuzzy
little bridge framed upon his wall.

Our Best-Kept Secrets

Our best-kept secrets
cover asses
cloud the mind
and fog up glasses.
But in the end
they are revealed,
for secrets worm
their way unsealed
out from the can.
And so those acts
catch up with us,
now or later
when we're dust.
We cannot ever win
with secrets held
within,
though many try
and many die
thinking they've
succeeded.

The Pilgrimage

Illness and obligations
keep him on another shore,
but
he came back to visit briefly
one time more
this town,
his town,
where his heart and past
are kept,
wrapped up in a prayer.
He knelt and prayed
upon his parents' grave,
and looked out from the Church
to see the diamond city
winking back at him
in love and admiration,
blinking back the tears
of this,
perhaps the last,
goodbye.

(About His Holiness Pope John Paul II's
visit to Krakow, Poland.)

The Iceman "Cameth"

The ice man came
in the waning cool
of morning,
lifting cold, huge blocks
upon his thick, bare shoulder,
chipping off a sliver for us
"little shavers" running after,
laughing,
wanting so to be just like him
when we all grew up.
. . . I wonder where
the iceman is today.

Relatively Speaking

He's been the first
to read all the "best" books
and see every "quality" film,
and he lets you know
with his critical reviews
and superior advice that
he's an "intellectual" who's
got it all figured out,
you poor slob!

(Maybe not in so many words,
but you get the point).

The Power of the Word

"Little movies"
are the poems I write:
opening scenes
to a different life
where boundaries
don't exist,
where smells and sounds
and sights all twist
and rise together
like the smoke
that curls up from
a shaman's pipe,
where lives take flight
within
the power of the word.

Destinations

Strangers crossing paths -
travelling on the highways,
subways, airways.
And whether it's for work
or play
we always seem
to speed away
to another destination.
Will we ever know
just what it is
we're running from?

Spider Woman

Spider woman
glides
on gossamer strands
from here to her eternity,
securing egg sacs and
not looking back
on the loving mate
she ate for lunch.

Living River

Living river flows,
rushes on its way
tearing endlessly
at the sandy sides
where dark things hide
buried in deep ignorance,
will wash them all away
grain by grain
until bare rock peeks out
again
all stripped and glistening.

And on and on
the river flows,
also covering things
as it goes. . .
    . . . living river!

Aunt Pearl

Aunt Pearl leads
a black and white existence
on the outside
with her plain talk
drab clothes
sensible shoes
hair going gray and
gravity having its way.
But, in her crazy inner home
she lives embraced
by her imagination,
and her mind is snapping
vivid prints
all the time,
all in Kodachrome.
And if you follow
the twinkle in her eye
you could end up
right inside the middle of
one of her "Kodak Moments".

The Tank

The "tank" in which I sat
in my imaginary war
did look shell-shocked
(just like me),
but really was a rusty,
dented heap.
I played my games
of make-believe in there,
though at the time
they seemed so real,
so gory,
that I got completely lost
inside the metaphor.

The Ignominious Demise
of Lady Sarah

Clothed in such frippery as velvet bustle
and buttonholed boots,
cutting a fine figure
as she crossed the kitchen and herself,
she poured out a crocodilian potion
in volute crystal,
as the vultures behind her wall
watched the sludge form
at the bottom of the glass,
counting the minutes
that lagged behind
the impending dirty deed.
And where, pray tell, was her god?

Filters

Many layers
gauges, sizes
protect us
from the noises
and events
that try to
shock us,
rock us from
our firm
foundations.

My Old Shoes

My old shoes
sure don't look like much
leaning up against
the closet resting -
dusty, scuffed and
thin-soled,
leather bulging,
having bent themselves
right out of shape for me.
And _they_ know
where we've been and
who we've seen,
and all the secrets in between
the comings and the goings.
But they won't tell,
having laced their tongues
up tight -
my dear old shoes!

Solutions?

In the quiet cool of the morning,
still embraced by fragments
of a dream that bubble up
"SOLUTIONS"
in mellifluous voice,
(which likely will elude me later
when I'm wide awake
and "thinking" -
or be revealed as garbage),
life seems controllable
and constant.
But, even in this dreamlike state
deep down I sense
the only constant thing about me
is the beating of my heart,
and <u>nothing</u> is controllable.
But still, I drift along,
loath to leave the sweetness
of that honeyed tongue.

Writing In the Moment

My poems are not me
I tell myself, and you.
I must stay free
behind the words I write,
the ones that strive
to tell you how I feel
right now -
not yesterday,
not tonight, and surely
not tomorrow.
So, don't cement me
in those thoughts I share
with you,
for I'm describing feelings
only passing through,
although they're absolutely true
this very moment.

Children Having Babies

Children having babies,
knowing little of the world
knowing little of themselves.
Lost within a world of cries
and dirty diapers,
childhood ends.

Weeping Walls

Half a teardrop stretches
down an ancient wall
moss-grown
wind-blown
far from anyone at all.
And why do old walls weep?
Why, from the secrets
that they keep.

Pressure Cooker

Lift the lid
of this pressure cooker -
we've stewed here
long enough;
we're pretty tough
by now.
And how
do tender hearts
turn tough?
Just let them simmer
in their own juice
long enough.

Duke's
("Best Buns On the Beach")

Wood shavings on the floor,
people out the door
lining up for "bitchin' burgers"
Kona chili
killer chili cheese fries.
Aromas from the grill invite
and booths await in red and white.
A shark's head juts out through the wall,
showing off its gleaming bite.
An old red Schwinn and surfing gear
hang with ukeleles, ads for beer.
"Woodies" stand out from the wall
among the pictures and the shirts
that advertise it all.
A pleasant din surrounds
with jukebox sounds of rock and roll
TV sports, a game of pool
mingling with the friendly chatter
from the crowd
in this little home away from home:
Duke Kahanamoku would be proud!

The Locket

The locket that she wore
was worn by others long before -
though not in her own family.
The precious heart
of burnished gold
had in ages past been
handed down, then sold,
to buy bread for a family
that had fallen on hard times:
father gone
children hungry
mother desperate.
But, the locket cannot tell
that tale, although the picture
inside hidden, pale,
shows a lady laced and proud
peering out.
No smile there, as
was the custom of the day,
no words appear to say just
who she was or how she felt, or
what her life was all about
before the locket travelled
to another heart.

Just Waiting For the Muse

No name
no thought,
no bright idea,
just waiting for the muse
to reappear
and light a fire
under my butt.
But, you know what?
Sometimes I wait
a hellava long time.

A Potato Truck

A potato truck
peeling through a skin of darkness
slides on a slick and winding road.
Around the corner it loosens its load,
and the tarp once closed
snaps past its rope restraints.
Spuds roll out singly, then in waves,
with eyes agog at their escape.
Potatoes going everywhere!!
Mashed on the windshields
of the cars behind,
drivers panic, driving blind.
A dark comedy, this, for the headline
on the front page read:
"Captive Spuds Attempt Escape -
Several Dead".

Dream-Clouds

The clouds are oozing
slowly
through a turquoise sky
today,
as if squeezed from tubes
of celestial toothpaste.
And as they pass
in feathered plumes
and mackerels,
as earthly creatures
or strange images quite magical,
this puff parade
evolving and dissolving
teases us
to leave one dream
and enter another.

Give and Take, Take

He is Friday
and cool water to my soul.
He embraces all my dreams
and mingles with my ghosts.
And as I float upon a sea
of cold indifference,
I slowly break through
waves of selfish thoughts
to wonder if
I give him back enough.
The stark, cold answer
splashed upon my face
is always . . .
. . . no.

The Stuntman

The stuntman
takes the fall for others,
paid to keep
those pretty bodies
perfect and intact.
He wears their bruises
and their cuts
like badges.
But
I wonder what
the tough guy's feeling
deep inside
beneath his wounds.
Does he hide a softer side -
one that cries
when no one's in the room?

The Celluloid Cowboy

With legs as tall
as the Empire State Building
he strides across the silver screen.
And with a jingle of spurs
and crooked grin
he projects upon the wall
the boldest dreams
we hold within.

On the Mesa

On the mesa
shadows dance in moonlight glow.
I hear footsteps, see the imprints
in the soft, volcanic stone.
And the night wind whispers gently
through the pines and tufa canyons,
stirring up the cottonwoods
stirring up my soul,
as I am drawn into a world
where spirits come and go.

The Wolf

The wolf sits still
on heavy haunches,
head back
howling to a silver moon.
And I wonder:
do his cries end there?
Or, is he sending
canine litanies of prayer?

In ___ We Trust

Raised in a house
where God was not
discussed
(in ___ we trust),
the questions in her
little mind
bounced back and forth,
remained unanswered
over time.
And then one day
she knelt before
death's door and
tried to pray.
Only then she saw the
bloody-handed image
reach across her mind
and close the door.

This Nose

This nose
stuck in the middle
of my face
has always had
this size and shape,
and my eyes are
used to peering out
around it.
Well . . . except for when
my nose gets out
of joint, and swells
across my face,
obstructing sight.
That's when I wonder
if I've got the right
proboscis!

The Lotus

The lotus rises from the mud
majestic, proud,
never gazing down,
as it looks beyond
the tread of man and beast.
And
thus in purity does it keep
its heavenly endowments
safely sealed
within its soft, white lips.

Toadstools

A silent fungal army
pops up in the storm,
bouncing raindrop
bullets
from its fleshy
helmets,
(really little tuffets
waiting for the sun
and wee Miss Muffets).

The Disappearance

No one knows what happened
to the man.
We all suppose he must be dead
by now
for it's been decades, after all,
since they found his shoes and wallet
on the beach
complete with money and
some pictures of his wife and kids.
No one knew that he was in despair
so the answers to our questions
have evaporated into thin air,
just like him!

Where Are We Going?

Today, feeling tired and drained,
I go on, having been trained
to put one foot
right in front of the other.
And through my tears
I see my mother,
thirty years of steps ahead of me,
still putting her best foot
forward.
Can you tell me, Mom,
where we are going?

I don't want much:
I just want a masterpiece.

(Any time now
would be fine.)

The Green Room

The green room's where
my Dad's Dad sat
and smoked his pipe
and read in vested silence.
I met him once
when I was five
and was invited up
into his sanctuary.
There I smelled his smokey air
and watched the dusty sunbeams
settle on his rolltop desk.
Time seemed to stop between us
as we sat in old stuffed chairs
and sipped our tea
and talked of "grown-up" things.
I never saw him after that,
but the photo that I snapped
was clear:
    he sits there still
    and smiles
    and chats with me,
year after changeless year.

The Arrowhead

In my hand I hold the weapon
of another time.
It's obsolete, but just as deadly now
as in its prime.
Aloud I ask this black and shiny
piece of glass,
"How many victims did you claim
before you killed your last?".
But
silence shrouds this little piece of history,
leaving us to contemplate the mystery.

Mary Tucked Inside

The amaryllis,
opening minutely day by day,
demurely,
even though she is
a Naked Lady
without a cloak to cover up
her pink unfolding lips,
gives the viewer
silent lessons
in the practice of seduction.

I Am One of Legions

I am one of legions
marching,
marching to an
evolutionary drummer,
marching throughout time.
And though you feel me,
(and my siblings),
you will never see me
eye to naked eye:
I travel differently,
in quite non-human style.
But, we are linked together,
you and I,
for when your life is over,
so is mine.

- The Virus

Bedbug

Today I'm in bed
with a bug,
(not a nice companion),
who's tickling my throat
and stuffing my nose.
No fair, Bug!
You're nestled
in my covers
warm and cozy,
while I sneeze and
blow, and beg you
to go away.
And you,
you little pest,
just rattle my chest
with your laughter.

He Pushed Me

He pushed me to the limit
and beyond.
And at the time
I wasn't very fond of him,
swinging as he did
his verbal hatchet
right between my eyes.
He called it therapy.
I called it cruel.
But psychic surgery
did prevail, and
I am living proof.

When They Peered

When they peered
into her mind,
doctors fully trained
could find just thoughts
recoiling,
scampering off like mice
before the traps were set.
So before the docs
could get a sample
for the biop,
they had to stop
their digging
and go buy cheese.

Threads

Those threads that bridge across
the waves
and reach beyond the grave
link family chains that stretch
unbroken
eons back beyond our memories,
rattling any family skeletons
hiding still
in dusty, genealogical closets.
And even if we try ignoring
this strong linkage with the past,
we can't escape the end results
of hands
that helped to shape us.

Miracles

Water
and
chemicals
hugged by
membranes
dividing it all
into countless cells,
somehow get it together
and make us what we are.
Now,
don't you believe in miracles?

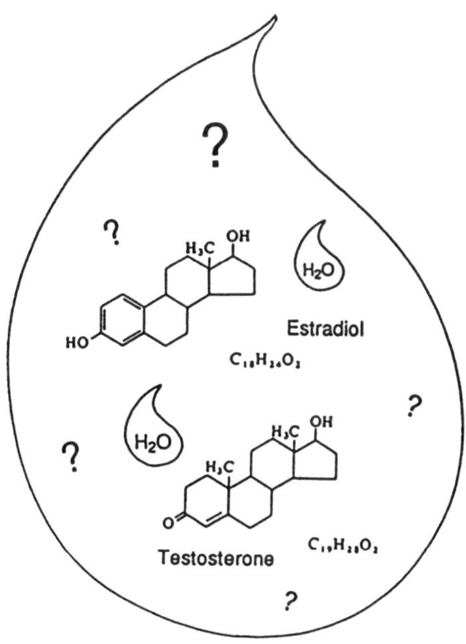

The Healing

The healing came slowly,
covering up in time
that fine red line
drawn from the past,
a past that nearly killed
the future.

The Vase

This dainty little vase
that holds a solitary rose
is hand-blown Swedish glass
recently discovered
in a pile of trash, and
rescued mud-caked but intact.
And as I sit and dwell upon
its unknown past,
it rests there quietly,
arms around the rose, and
sparkles in the silence.

Dream-Child

Charging after the image
of the child,
laughing, naked, and wild,
and with each blink
I think he's run a little farther
from my reach -
blond hair, flying silk
in breezes blowing out beyond me.
Dream-child!
Do your sea-green eyes now flash
upon another landscape?
Don't you remember,
only yesterday we ran laughing
through the meadow
soft and green before the mowing?
Dream-child?
Wait!

My Cats

My cats
nap, pounce, swat and hiss
wrestle, chase, then make-up kiss
gobble food in perfect bliss
take daily baths in their own spit,
curl, stretch, purr and yawn
sleep in sunshine, heads on paws,
watch the lizards and the birds,
complain that indoor life's absurd
scratch and sniff then play and tire
meeow to me their deep desires.
And when I'm sick or feeling lonely,
they come in and will leave only
when I'm better,
for my cats are loyal friends,
and I love them both.
The End.

In a Verdant Glade

In a verdant glade I sit,
in shady coolness by a stream
    and rest my weary brow.

I watch the gentle water glide
and gurgle by, and so it seems
    to talk to me somehow.

I drink in all the sweetness of
each clear and bubbling word,
    as it passes by.

And I strain to comprehend, as
somewhere in my soul is heard
    every gentle sigh.

This language I have heard before.
I knew it many years ago,
    and I have felt a stirring

of a memory lodged within
my mind, and in my soul a glow,
    which is now recurring.

The Bad Dream

The bad dream grew
by leaps and bounds
into a nightmare
that shook me sweating
from the bed.
Relieved I wasn't dead,
I headed straight
for the kitchen
to celebrate my lucky fate
with the contents
of the refrigerator.

Old Home Movies

Old home movies
flicker,
skip across the screen, and
it sure seems like only yesterday
(or was it just a dream?)
when we were all that young,
when long-gone relatives
and friends
were still alive, and
when we thought we'd all survive . . .
. . . forever.

Shadow Woman

Shadow Woman
orchestrates
a symphony of moons, and
incubates her precious seeds
in living pools.
They grow to viciousness
sometimes,
lashing back at her.
But unknown to them
she lives within, and
therefore will endure.

Man, the lofty
thinker's
also
Man, the dirty
stinker.

Killing Time

I'm "killing time"
but
the joke's on me,
for
day by day,
time's killing <u>me</u>.

Careful kicking
   around ideas,
      for one may
         jump
right back
      and bite you
         where you
            least expect.

Skiing At Night

The silence wraps around us
like a fist
as night holds tight its breath
while we slide through it:
Swish! Swish!
So cold
so still
so beautiful this land
where moonbeams turn
the landscape into silver crust,
covering up that mortal dust
which hides our dreams.

The Pepper Tree

Perched high in
　　the pepper tree
　　　　no windows, doors,
　　　　　　with roof that leaks
　　　　　　　　a special house exists for me.

Hiding in my
　　special place
　　　　where ants and sap
　　　　　　stick hands and face,
　　　　　　　I feel safe.

For I can take my
　　troubles there,
　　　　and dreams of future
　　　　　　I will share
　　　　　　　　with the pepper tree.

And lacy branches
　　nod and sigh
　　　　as they hold me
　　　　　　when I cry
　　　　　　　　in the pepper tree.

The Ginger Jar

The ginger jar
is where she keeps her dreams
a quarter at a time,
(in bad weeks just a dime).
She envisions life anew,
a place to call her own
without the chips and scratches
or the nasty landlard
of her past.
She glues her eyes
upon a distant shore, and
builds her bridge now
board by board.

The Undertaker

The undertaker
grins from deep within.
He hides behind
his neat moustache
and unctuous words.
With a fine Italian suit
and white carnation
adding to his careful sense
of pale, groomed elegance,
he looks remarkably like
his horizontal clients.

The Old Photo

Frozen in time
I see him
    mid-glance
    mid-smile
young face peering
out at mine,
a little boy
long
before my time.
I later called him
    "Dad".

The Old-Fashioned Dolls

The old-fashioned dolls
sitting upon my shelf
are tiny, porcelain toys
that have survived
my mother's childhood.
One wears homemade dress
and pants -
the other one wears nothing
but a thoughtful glance.
They look askance now
at each other's painted face,
perhaps frozen
in some silent memory
of the trials and tribulations
of a little girl who had no
chance to finish childhood play.

The Grandchild

The grandchild growing
in its mother's sea,
floating warm and toasty,
is a miracle unfolding.
And we who on the outside
wait in great anticipation
already love this precious
little combination of us all,
who because of that,
remains unique. Godspeed!

The Clock Tower

The whirring
of the well-oiled
gears,
(music to the
watchman's ears),
tick-talk the seconds
into years
in clock-time.
And
paying never-mind
to God or man,
they urge the clock
to run its hands
across the face
of time.

Killing Fields

Beehives
of hard-hatted activity
buzz,
as Caterpillars
crawl upon the earth
and raze,
eradicate all beauty.
And some will call this
"progress"
as the land is scraped clean
like a plate,
to nakedly await
the final blow,
the one that buries it alive
and far below
the concrete shrouds
of man.

Leaves and Lessons

Leaves twist and strain
upon the branch
turning red and veined
with all that effort.
Finally
chilling winds of autumn
come and pluck them free.
And, as they drift
and tumble down
to earthy waiting arms,
they taste a freedom
which would never come
by hanging on.

Cowboys

Cowboys
now a dying breed,
squint-eyed watch
their world recede
as plains and badlands
shrinking fast
slip out from their
calloused grasp,
sinking back into a past
of dusty legends
all around them.

Standing In the Shower

Standing in the shower
lost within the steam,
lost within the power of a dream
where all the water
leaked beneath my skin,
and swirling deep within my
darkest places,
(never reached before
and never seen),
the warm wet needles
swept me clean.
And leaving no bone dry,
no cell untouched,
the water quickly reached my soul,
where in it gushed,
to finally wash away the
pain and lingering doubts
of yesterday.

Jessie

She was sexy and fastidious
with every hair in place
in the cool of the morning,
(though she never knew the day
or time, but that didn't matter).
And even the delicate drool
that escaped her lips
dared not to drip in fractious
pools.
She had to be completely
in control,
(if only an illusion).

They Won't Be Seen Till Halloween

The witch on the broom with the cat,
and the moon
all swirled together in the month of June
in a magic spell
that (if all goes well)
will bring them back quite changed
and sober,
sometime around the end of October.
So, please stay tuned!

Special Bells

Some bells which toll
are seen by me
alone
for they are special bells
which swing
within a solitary tower,
locked away from view
locked away from you.
And
though I see them clearly
swaying neatly measured
like a clock
even _I_ must strain to hear
their pure, rich tones
ringing from the inside out.

Tidal Wave

That tidal wave of accusation
crashing from your mind
did catch me unaware that time,
did find a shore to batter and destroy.
And in the eerie calmness after,
rolling in on silent foam,
I finally felt your eyes hold mine.
And though your lips did not apologize,
I did accept one from your eyes.

The Drill Sergeant
(Among Other Things)

Yesterday I met an iceberg
of a woman.
The tip
above the surface
fooled me for a while.
But soon I realized that
her thoughts ran deep, that
she was quite unique
in her accomplishments.
And, as she chipped off chunks
below the surface,
offering up
(just bit by bit)
each tantalizing piece
of her complexity,
I stood there frozen,
quite astounded by her list:
scientist and mother,
teacher and photographer,
and . . . oh, yeah,
soft-spoken-tough drill sergeant
in the United States Marines!

Stone Lanterns

Stone lanterns
keep their guard
along a gravel walk
that winds and beckons
to a temple high above
the minds of men,
while
in the sandy fields below
God's latent prints remain,
kept locked away
in lacquered boxes
in the brain.

Never Thought I'd Say

Never thought I'd say
I miss the cold of winter -
the crunch of feet in snow
eyelashes iced together
faces all aglow,
making "angels" in a woods
chilled into silence,
sledding
laughing down a hill
and landing at the bottom
in a heap.
And later on, bright cheeks and
hot spiced cider all around
the fire.
Oh, yeah . . .
        . . . and,
digging ice off windshields
in a freezing rain,
sliding on an icy road,
shoveling snow
hands frozen to the bone
body sweating
glasses steamed.

Did I say
I miss the cold of winter?

Snow

Snow blows chill
upon the wind and white,
and sparkles day and night
like the gleam in your eye,
like pure cane sugar from Hawaii
(the refined kind).
And each flake,
separate and unique,
would tell (if it could speak),
a different story.

- D.R. Bach

Dragonflies

Swirling
hovering in a swarm
twoscore and more
fill the sky.
It's impossible to count
these dipping, diving
kamikazes
crimson, iridescent flashes
plunging
just above a pepper tree
which seems to hold
this living cloud
tightly to itself
like a magnet.

In the Studio

The palettes, easel,
floor and walls
wear rainbow splatters
glowing
in the dawn's first light.
Smells of turpentine
and oils
mingle with the coffee,
boiled,
mingle with the
"wake-up call".
And the master yawns
while stretching
canvas all around the edges
of a frame
that will display
a fragment of his brain
today.

Making Plans

While I was busy
making plans
my life occurred.
It happened quickly
so the facts are blurred.
And still I'm stuck
in planning mode,
even though by now
the whole dam load
has shifted into middle age.
It seems I just can't learn -
I don't know why.
But, prob'ly I'll be
making plans the day I die.
(You may have my plans
then, if you like.)

A Protozoan Profile

The amoeba moves
ahead
behind besides,
(no bones about it),
oozing along in pools of
pseudopodic exploration.
And though it's just a simple
one-celled creature,
it nonetheless displays
those very features
of the vital life process
which
the rest of us possess.

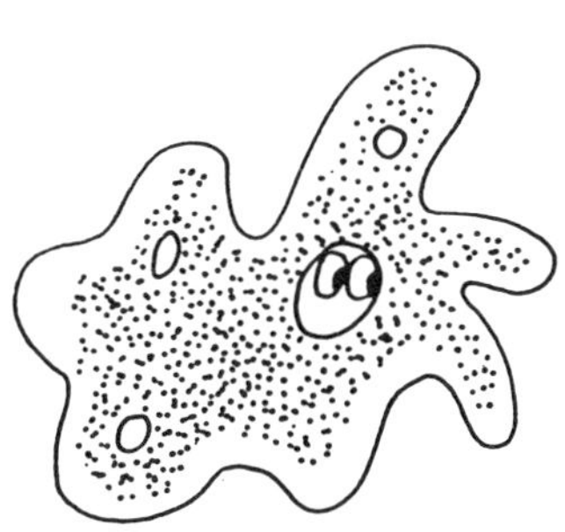

Moving Mountains

The weathered granite lips
(rock solid) that do
heavenward reach up
to kiss
those whipped-cream puffs
that float between
those other worlds
and us,
do hold a tenderness within
their stoney prisons.

Passing Through

Passing through
the eye of a needle, or
tripping to the Dog Star,
going wherever your mind
will take you -
you'll find these journeys
not impossible or far.
The benefits of mind travel
much outweigh the pain,
and the loss in orientation
is ultimately your gain
as you begin
to experience
worlds
once thought
unattainable.

Web of Desire

Web of desire
Nebulous
Sticky-fingered threads
Holding on to hope, as
Heart-fires burn and
Weld the strands together.
Haphazard junctures
Unlikely unions
Married in a crazy quilt of
Love and pain and longing.
Cartwheeling web
Spinning through space
Out of reach
Out of sync
But brightly shining
Teases us to follow
In our clumsy way.

I Am Purple Passion

I am purple passion
bottled up in hand-blown glass.
I am pink trouble on wobbly legs.
I am a mountain cliff
where nothing grows but the wind.
I am a frozen waterfall, but
soon will be the songbird's drink.
I am a place beyond known places.
I am the open door
of tomorrow's promise -
(I promise)!
I am a deep-purple onion so sweet,
you fail to remember
I can make you cry.
I am the kindling that starts your fire.
And you -
you are the ocean and the stars,
the sweet breath from the woods,
and all the tender hearts combined.

The Recital

She told me not to "sweat it"
but I sit and wait with
butterflies
and hands that shake,
rubber knees,
and even when
I think, "Be cool!"
my hands begin to sweat,
and I'll just bet
the teacher's nervous, too!

The Giant Hook

The giant hook
of your affection
has hoisted me aloft
and kept me dangling
high above
the mirrors of my mind,
high above
those humming gears
which easily can grind
me into dust
with just the slightest
provocation.

Cousin Frank's Eddy

In a dream I fell right off
the edge of time
as thoughts exploded
from my mind and landed
in the eddy cousin frank
stirred idly with a straw
(in chocolate milk, no less).
And
then I saw frank's thoughts
dive in and swirl around
with mine
within that milky pool
until he sucked them up again
into oblivion.
And though I know
t'was just a dream
I've lately found it hard
it seems
to stomach cousin frank.

Freudian Slippers

Wearing my Freudian slippers,
I pad about and try to analyze
my life (and yours) in great detail,
searching for a soul
or at least an answer or two.
And without fail I find discrepancies
that blaze a trail right to the nearest
bookstore's "self-help" section
where I buy
the latest shiny-covered panacea.
And though a lot of what I read
just seems absurd, I never learn:
I keep on buying every novel word.
I guess the "gurus" have _me_ analyzed:
they somehow figured out
my Freudian slipper size!

Growing Older Together

I gaze across the Cheerios
at your dear face,
(craggy reflection of my own wrinkles),
that face I've seen now daily
for two decades plus,
with blue eyes just as sharp as ever, and
as you read the paper,
buttering your toast, I realize
we have been far luckier than most,
sharing loving bites and nibbles
along the way
with crumbs of laughter
sprinkled liberally around the pain.
And, do you know what?
I wouldn't have had it any other way.

The Homecoming

They say you can't go home again,
and maybe that's true for some,
(like I used to think it was true for me).
But, you know what?
"They" were wrong:
I did it!
It wasn't easy to find my way,
for I had been long gone.
And the forest had grown thick
with thorns and unwise choices.
So I got stuck, and I got cut, but
I finally did come out alive
on the other side.
It's true the town looked different
from before,
but deep within
where hearts and souls reside,
everything had stayed
pretty much the same.
I was welcomed back
as if I'd never left.
But I was different now,
having found some wisdom
along the way:
I'd returned now unafraid
of my old ghosts.

About the Author

This is the second book of poetry published by Jackie
Bach. Her first book, <u>Through The Bach Door</u>, has been
very well received, especially by those who have
struggled with depression. Jackie is a survivor, and
she shows in her poems how writing can help one
recover from personal crisis. Her unique observations
are thought-provoking and often humorous. Many
readers have found that her poetry provides a trigger
for talking about their own feelings. And since Jackie's
poetry is thoroughly accessible, it has been
appreciated even by the "nonpoetry lover".
In addition to Jackie's talents as a writer and artist,
she is a musician and teacher of piano, violin, flute,
and guitar. She graduated Phi Beta Kappa from the
University of Michigan in 1975.
Jackie lives in Southern California with her husband
and two "therapist" cats.